Writings

I0162766

From

The

Well

By: Brian Sewell (*The Native*)

Writings From The Well

Printed in America

ISBN-13:978-0692302972
ISBN-10:0692302972

Printed by Createspace 2014
Published by BlaqRayn Publishing Plus 2014

What Do We Teach Her

What do we teach her..Looking for reflection but if there's an absent mother those demons through the screen may reach her...She may choose to use her body instead of her mind..She may go without the knowledge to things done there is no rewind...She may run the streets instead of track...She may allow life to color her heart black...What do we teach her.....Award shows show scantly clad women dancing for many eyes to see...But she looks up to them saying "its like them I want to be"..Lyrics tell her the body is no temple but an instrument to be put to their use..Slowly the pressure of their beckoning will tighten the noose...What do we teach her...A baby is a paycheck...There's no such thing as self respect...What do we teach her...When will we teach her...Who is it we are letting teach her?..Their saying your ass is your future so make sure its showcased...Be less focused on the shaping of your heart and more on your face...At a certain age we wonder why we cant reach her...But what do we teach her..

Someone To Love Her

She just wants somebody to love her..To
always be thinking of her..Until then she seems
satisfied with the late night roaming..On
another man's sheets she'll be moaning...To
awake for early am departure..As she living
room lounges with wine awaiting that well
known archer..A few shots grazed her but true
penetration was long ago..And true love seems
to be the only feeling she wants to
know..Until ...then shes warmed by the
embrace of alcohol..A veteran of last call...The
mentality of a man...I got what i wanted from
him because i can...and it felt good...Its a
matter of what i want not a matter of if I
should...But behind blinds alone she just wants
someone to love her...And not just under a
cover...A man that will play her game of waiting
and not let their moments be premature...She
wants to be sure...That he'll love her...But until
then she calls up another friend who's down for

late night escaping into the ecstasy...Maybe all that watching her life affected me...Because I know...she just wants somebody to love her...

Sweet Mistakes

Necessary….to carry the past on my shoulders like boulders…Or so I thought until I bought better sense n awoke to fresh scents like Folgers…They want me to be there…Wrapped in carefree sheets in the heat of the next tear..To torn…Maybe the best of me was just worn…Memories are sure to fade of the spots where I've laid…In beds of sick heads I brought no aide…The basic instincts used to leave you gratefully used or bitterly abused…Speaking on things you could only do boozed…I asked where is the love?…A voice whispered beyond the flesh you crave that's enslaves what your speaking of….Scents and rooms that become tombs of sweet mistakes…

Race War

I'm seeing another civil war..Another color
death has the country tore...Its going back to
the time before..but its no secret this place has
an unremoved sore..called racism..And they
want us to hate with em...What a shame all that
work done in vain..The plans have been laid
plain..Separate the people in groups so we can
send out troops for more killing...Instead of
uniting for a cause for nothing ...they'll die
willing...Check world-star...Or a country
bar...Shared videos of fighting among
ourselves its a shame...all that work done in
vain...It was headed towards rich vs poor..But
it wont be that way anymore...I see another
civil war coming..Can almost hear those
marchers drumming...To deaths tune...And it
wont even be high noon before they
draw..Shots fired...They don't imprison
crooked cops they just get fired..Meanwhile
they'll fire at colored people as we fire at

ourselves…Because no one reads those eye
opening books sitting on shelves…I see
another civil war coming… Because instead of
being united we just keep running…from the
truth…Its time to come together for
change..Before armed men on corners no
longer seems strange…

Power To The People

Power to the people indeed. Power to the people forever. To the tribes of stolen lands brutalized from the coasts to the plains to those crammed on ships n formally wrapped in chains....We must flow together with these words to shake the slumber from their brains...And pump the life giv...ing truth into their veins....To rise and knock from their throne the elite group that reigns...Walk through parts of the South you may still see the blood stains..From where men women and children were hanged...Beaten to death or gun shot banged...You'll still see the broken buildings where native children were forced to unlearn their culture..Follow the trail of tears where they cut open pregnant women and left the remains for a circling vulture/Forced only to identify with who they were while losing ourselves...Its time to dig deep within our wells...Forced only to identify with "masters"....Called demons and savages by the pastors..We were never considered equal..Oh but in school they'll make you recite "We the people"...They gave us broken lands that became concentration camps they call reservations...A broken people of scattered nations...But on the lit box they only show the casino..But we know..the truth...We need to reteach our youth..We need to not be spread apart like fingers but come together to form the fist..We need to do more than just exist..We must rise together or fall apart...Power to the people indeed....Power to the people forever...

Roses and Rain

ROses and RAin..She smelled like roses and rain...was so vain but at my every advance she came as we danced in the light of the moon in that room of the basement..She came with kisses for my pain and its hard to explain how a simple name can send shock waves of blame down through each finger point reaching for a joint asking was she heaven sent?..I'm all but bent to breaking for mistaking myself as right in a wrong doing as I tell myself I was young..Trading the joint for an L as the smoke swells in my lung..lungs..Listening to words from different tongues on how distance won't work and was a jerk for listening...But I still remember her body glistening...Smelling like...ROses and RAin to ease my pain but the same woman sat in tears while her fears came the same...Because of listening to peers I brought her fears and was to blame..For the same story of a dude trading one for another because his other might have known another brother..Somehow after all the years I still love her..As I "burn out" my pain..Wondering if she still smells like ROses and RAin...And now these brainstorms are watering the pages of my notebook as I take a window look to clear weather....forever...forever?...forever...a word I said plenty without any head time but through young lips it sounded better..and its now or never time but..I rhyme of a time better...Starbucks stains and Amtrak trains..Blood rushed veins as we kissed all pains..We spent cold nights close until warm became familiar...and I would do anything to once again feel her...anything....anything... Forever burned into my brain to be the brand of my pain..forever again wishing to be washed in ...roses and rain....

Carry Yourself

I could tell you…everything they will…I could let those flowing compliments spill…Onto your canvas of thought to create what you desire to see..But that just wouldn't be me…I'd rather tell you to carry yourself with the respect you wish to receive or you will be treated as the image you allow to be perceived…Be careful the motivation you allow to lead…you…A woman who says a man made …me this way allows said man to become her maker forever bent by his design…I hope there is never around your neck a sign..Saying for sale…Because there is no such thing as bought love only rented time for when money is the motivation love will always fail…Listen close I'm not trying to spin a tale I am only trying to tell the truth..Look on the television for the proof…They have made you an object of physical pleasure and if you dress the part they think you'll play the role..Don't let your inner beauty be stole….n…By a man who just wants to get in..Or your morals fall for last call or a group of friends down to lose it all...I could tell you..everything they will..I could let those flowing compliments spill...Onto your canvas of thought to create what you desire see..But I'd rather tell you to carry yourself with the respect you wish to receive.or you will be treated as the image you allow to be perceived....

Glass Mirrors

We chase good feelings to the bottom of bottles
only to stare at our empty reflection...Moments
of clarity for self inspection...I wonder at the
findings discovered..All that pain uncovered..Its
the true artists that hold the deepest scars...I
guess that's why u may find so many of us
attending bars...To wash out our wounds...

Suicide Queen

A night of pouring has her head full..As eager lips take a pull…from whatevers lit…Another hit..Another tab from a downtown scene with changing characters that perform the same acts ..She never retracts…those things said to another well dressed stranger whose eyes are aimed at her lack of covering…That poisons effect has started the smothering…of any good choices..It wont matter after she leaves she never hears their voices…Another night of pouring has her head full and her bed full…another pull…of whatevers lit…Hanging from her decisions but only when she stops kicking can she quit…The Suicide Queen

A Walk Through The Neighborhoods

I've been through the neighborhoods where
children roam with no watchful eye of guardian
in sight..Where pools of toxic substance drown
the care of fathers..Where mothers sell
themselves for another hit...Where a long look
can mean trouble..Where the police are a
cause for fear...Where the mixed sounds of
cries and sirens will have you believing God
is ...nowhere near..My friend told me he saw
the devil on a corner..The same one
elementary school girls dance to music blaring
"twerk bitch"...Where the tap water sippers
have dreams of being rich...I've been through
the neighborhoods where the ones carrying
books are beat on...Where jokes are like pain
pills..Where there's one girl with too many
mistakes...But there was no one to teach
her...Where the whole community lets their
hopes ride on the athletic boy...I've been
through the neighborhoods where politics is

another word for rich liars in suits…Where the
flag is a symbol of oppression..Where outside
of the school you may learn the biggest
lesson…Where the gas station is the gate to
"feel good"…I've been through the
neighborhoods raised by vulgar words and
violent movies..Hard times…I've been through
the neighborhoods…in need of
teachers…preachers…and hope…Where the
government started pumping the dope…Where
police beat men and women the same…Where
they make you state aloud your changed
name….Where the trick of it all started at the
beginning..I've been through the
neighborhoods..created to keep us down

The
Mended Heart

Every moment...Every moment at your side I
enjoy the ride...Whether our energies are
flowing in a direction or sitting still waiting for
the green light....So we can go...But I'd stay
parked happily gazing at the scenery...that you
provide..Oh what a joy to be inside..your
waiting arms...Its so great that with you there
are no alarms...signaling danger..And knowing
that belonging to you many dangers I will be
kept from...The past is a charred minefield of
self inflicted explosions...But you were the
medic waiting...Look at this beautiful war story
we've been creating...Victory beyond the
storm...And for me it came in such a beautiful
form...What a sight for sore eyes...The
greatest prize...
An unconditional love

Scattered Thoughts

Staring through a scope so that's tunnel vision as I peer at my visually realized vision that this place has become a prison..

My hope for man was high until I learned about that dope in the sky they fly and more than that the fact that freedom must be a conscious decision..

And in that I see from these children of men that were once free that that'...s a decision I may never see…

Because truly conscious again they may never be…

Subdued minds in the mines of rich devils…

My climb out of such started at a tree then it reached mountain tops in its levels…

I'm going deep so don't drown..

Once was lost but now I'm found they say let freedom ring n I ask can you hear the sound?….

Subdued minds in the mines of rich devils…

Your mind can be a beautiful rose...let no one
pluck the petals...

Speaking of plucking the thorns in my mental
need such...

Remembering the warmth of loves touch..

She said the words I love you more than you
can fathom...

But I could only reply I battle for hours in my
think tank and learned when backs are turned
that's the time people stab em...

Stone cold I've been told refusing to fold
because once you compromise yourself that's
when you are sold...

This new view is quickly getting old and my
inner me is quickly getting bold...

Heard it said I can't save these slaves from
ignorance's grip..

And heard it said your gone in your head you
need to get a grip...

He said this can't be just a phase because the
answers to your question lie beyond the maze..

Meanwhile I've debated falling out of loves for
days but before I do let me count the ways...
I forgot to button up so the world sees my
emotions open..Saying before I go you need to
know the truth will be spoken...

Point of View

We are infected by...the why try? point of view
and that is true..The curtains they've pulled
closed I see through..I seek too..More than the
average human being barely being in this state
of existence darkened by clouds of lacking
care..The right path is where?..I say often not
far from what you know and that your hearts
already told you so.....I may be a starter or a
martyr..Or a living testimony of the way not to
go but who lets himself be left at the harbor..As
the ship to heaven sails because at attempting
total goodness he only fails...Covered by a roof
but on me it daily hails..Ice cold blocks of
doubt..Interweaving two paths walking in and
out...To an ending route unknown with each
new truth uncovered by smothered lies my mind
is blown...I've grown apart from the world but
an umbilical cord of want still attaches me as if
by it I'm owned...Trying to tone the shape of my
heart so that its fit for love....I lost a beautiful

woman that few will know who I'm speaking of...As I reach above...To grip the hand of the true God who made me be...Yet it was the actions of mine that made me...Me....Now its that I see as I look into the mirror to find my soul...Behind eyes that the temperature of life made cold....We fight to never grow old but the sands of time blow for all mankind...As I seek to find...The truth of it all in the ties that bind....Seeing sheeple instead of people led blind....Where do I go from here?....Standing above hell hoping heaven is near....Hoping I can look over the fear...to see my way clear...

The Destruction of Innocence

Help me..she whispered a cigarette in one
hand the moist grip of the poison bottle in the
other...
Saturated in the watered down emotions of
loving another..
Losing hope with being able to cope veins dope
filled enough to smother..
Any thought of reaching...
...
Needing more than preaching...
Help me...
In the middle of misery brought on from a right
life gone left...
And now in the middle of misery she looks to
find whats left..
A broken soul that took a heavy toll from the
price of vice living...
And now laying in skin that's gone cold she
looks for a God forgiving..

Sex became a weapon even though it was used
to be a torment..

From the sick minds of relatives she was beat
and bent..

Bent an broken then sent back to her room in
tears chokin…

At times peering through blinds she wondered
would a kind word ever be spoken..

Now grown the past has shaped her unpleasant
present..

Selling her body for drugs and rent while living
as a peasant…

A slave to the "Feel Good" in her life of doing
what is so wrong…

She was hoping the birth of the last trash baby
would've brought freedom's song.…

Freedom meaning death as she lays in a daze
from a mental full of drugs…

From her father who wasn't such a father she
never looked forward to the hugs…

Another shot of hot liquid flame to ease the pain
from the abuse..
A life spent on death row begging for the
noose..
Once she dressed in a pretty dress now she
dresses only to play the part...
Pressed against the mirror snorting hope but
wishing for a fresh start..

In a world where good is against the fence and
most lack common sense...
I've watched the destruction of innocence...

Never Mine

Trapped on this roller-coaster of emotion
where my ups are sky high and my lows are
valley deep....
I remember without a peep at random times we
would creep...
Took your hand in mine and led you to a place
that felt divine..
Knowing the whole time that you were his and
never mine...
...
Maybe for a time but that time felt like a
moment...
I cherished every min...every second...each
component..
If time was for sale the time with you I'd love to
own it...
But every time your near I know its only for a
moment..
Crazy when the night feels right but bright of the
day burns wrong..

Crazy how it was you that someone like me
needed all along..
Traced each place on your skin as if I drew the
blue print..
Wondering in the moment if those things you
said you meant...
Feeling emotionally bent to a great extent with
these gaps in time....
Filling them in with the knowledge that you were
his....and never mine

Best Friend

Crazy how you always were her..the her that
I needed..Tear stains on my sleeve as I
breathe 100 degrees pass heated...Gimme
something to live for because since the
recent events I'm so unsure....Tripping over
the fact that I can never go back...Tripping
over the fact that those moments in time will
stay black...On the daily I would race to
your face and anywhere we went became a
special place....Intrigued by your special
taste double meaning since I never told you
I'm in love with the way you taste...Wait I
think I'm moving fast...But am I really since
its all in the past?....I just need to tell you
just how special you really are...Many lights
on this night but here your the only star.....I
miss the trips to the mall...And anytime you
tripped I had you before the fall...Truly you
were the only shoulder...And I was yours
too but your position made me

colder...Being second place to his face...The moments in between had me zoning in my space...But the smell of your scent brought me back....Genuine emotions with you I never had to act....Placed me on a different track and when I tell you that I love you its not a statement but a fact....The news of the move made me lose..Control....always wished it was you I could choose...console....Reflecting can be infecting to the soul....Making the wrong choice can take a heavy toll...Miles apart and still you have my heart...Miles apart and I still write you art...Can honestly say from the beginning to the end....I never knew I'd fall in love with my best friend.

Growing Up

She told him...call me when you stop writing
fairy tales boy...Chasing tails of pussy cats
playing with the strongest emotion like your
favorite toy...Maybe you'll never be grown...Or
find a feeling you can own...All those rented
emotions...They speak about you so loud I still
hear their commotions...And somehow I still
see more to you..Maybe I can see through
you...To your beating heart..If only you thought
with that from the start..But in-between
addictions...you write fictions...but hopefully
one day you'll think with your heart...so call me
when you start..

Love Things

She wished for all those things love was said to bring...They made it seem so sweet all those songs about it she'd sing...Every queen needs a king she thought...A mind full of fairy tales she'd been taught...No one told her about the games or the lies...No one told her how many times those late night songs would be the sounds of her cries...Because not all who come in the name of love will bear its mark on their heart....Some will even come to tear yours apart...But even after all the pain from the last sting...A new song she began to sing....wishing for all those things love was said to bring

Beautiful

I searched for beautiful and found it trapped within a bush of thorns...Checking twice at the sight for the possibility of hidden horns...But on my advance at a closer glance there was no creature at all...Just a fragile woman who had just about been through it all..I recall seeing this sight once before...yet I treated the holding of that beauty like a chore...And now the pain in my hands asks is this sight worth fighting for?...Blood stains on my skin from the prying to free her...Wondering if this struggle would lead us back to where we were...Trapped in thorns and hoping not to grow horns...Bleeding from my hands as I struggle to free...a sight that was just too beautiful to me...

For The Love of Money

Beginning to drown the sound of good so deep that the inviting melody of evil has lulled the people to sleep...Morally stripped industry producing an infantry of those no longer praying their soul to keep and the ones of old I've watched them weep...for our future...A tear in the mind of mankind that the ones who know seek to suture...In a stupor from the repetitive phrase that pays "cash rules everything around me" so for what gleams I may sell myself for my dreams..Have the times truly turned dark or is that just how it seems?...Wait....I ask is to grasp the hand weighted in rings become our fate?...

Drunk In Love

Then she said…I'm doing all the things I said I wouldn't do..couldn't do but lord knows the gauntlet these things have put her through.. N..now she's fondled again to bend to the floor…but her eyes avert to the door…Lips and limbs they beckon for more…But her hearts already so sore…Tore…No love in their lust n no room for the chore of trust…Trust…Shes downed those drinks to drown her do…wn…But the mistakes made after those drinks is what left her bound..She was so sure his love potion would pour n coat her heart to let her soar…But not anymore…Now in his leaving her grieving left her to with many footprints leading away from her door…Tore…Another drink to drown down that taste…Cupid's shot was a waste… Now the space between friend and lover is blurred to the point that no one knows…

Hiding the stains its the pain that shows...The girl who let go..

Empty Words

Promises...Often broken..Words said to the head not meant but often spoken..I find no comfort in lies they've never kept me warm..To some those lies become the norm...I've stayed inside along life's ride to avoid the storm..Because I know bad things can come in a beautiful form..My thoughts become bundles of green paper while seeking change..I felt the touch on my heart and it proved strange...Somewhere between balancing atop the crazy nest and holding onto sane..Tired of this pain..Promises..Often broken..Words said to the head not meant...but often spoken...

Questions

In a time where you tell a christian you can see demons and in their smirk you wonder what they believe in...All the smothering lies have me breathing heavy a bit unsteady in my pace but in the race for truth I'm speeding..Bleeding tears from the fears of things to come I wonder what will be the sum of their freedom..Wondering in my climb out from the grime of the world will I ever touch the kingdom...

I've been told I leak that speak people don't want to hear....If that's so maybe its the truth you fear..I was told long ago we all must make a choice then follow the choosing...And instead of seeking to find the reason to the rhyme some just stand accusing...

All the while the ones in power stand abusing...

And the resources of the world are running dry from the using...You can't claim an open mind

if you keep a closed door...Just when you think
you know enough....I promise you there's more

Clouds of Future

I see kings and queens caught in the same
twisted games while seeking fortune and fame
plus an echoing name but they lose themselves
in the seeking...Who is to blame? Is it the
vicious monsters of the industry no one will
stand to tame or the fact that the truth is
something few seem to be speaking...
Leaking...tears to cleanse my skin of the sin I
myself am stained with...Needing holy water for
the disorder that's come down but now society
has begun to view God as a myth...Oh what
have we come to?... Where will our children
run to?...The arms that once opened to love
are now drugged filled or closed for self
holding...A better future we need to be
molding...before its too late

Hate

Some of the greatest evils ever done were by men who said they did them for the greater good..They'd probably destroy half the world if they could..in the name of their cause..There is a predator lurking and it seeks to destroy everyone in the poison found in its jaws..What a horrible monster they did create..The beast called Hate...With all this blood spilling before my eyes its hard to concentra...te...Once bitten you will participate...in its bloodbath..But will never be able to cleanse yourself from the aftermath...it leaves behind..I heard nowadays its hard to find members of mankind who are colorblind..After all we are so grouped..So desperate to belong..to something...Even if that thing makes us condemn a man because of the way he was painted by his maker...Even if that group makes us a taker...of life...Or maybe even cut someone down with the blade of the sharpest knife...the human tongue...Oh

my i wonder from where this beast sprung...I
wonder who was its creator...The beast that
has made man a raper...a betrayer..an
emotion slayer..a land decimator...a taker....of
life...That will carve away care with the
sharpest knife....I just hope you don't make the
mistake...of being bitten by the beast...called
Hate

Dedication To My Brother

He probably thinks I'm forgetting him…After all so many have even after all the laughs n good times hes given them…But how could I?..How could I…His words are carved into the walls of my mind..Who do you think told me to seek to find?…Who do you think showed me the truth..Who do you think told me to show the proof..A legend who I'll speak about until I'm no longer here..I've never seen him… shed a tear…Even while enduring pain that would cripple giants and I've watched him slay a few..The missing body in the passenger seat has me wondering what to do..My journey is off balance..Every moment spent at his side is kind of tense…Because it may be the last one…I remember when we use to smoke loud packs down to the last one…I remember when the tube never left ESPN…I remember when I couldn't lose a grin…Because he held my spirit up for me…And I'd pay it all back if it was up to me..They probably never knew how badly he wanted to see his seeds...Or how often he regretted the past and his deeds...They probably never knew the demons that rode him...Or how no amount of physical pain could hold him...down...And even though hes still above ground....He probably thinks I'm forgetting him...but how could I?...He taught me more than any other...and he chose to be my brother....I told them I'll be legendary....because I sat with a legend.

About The Author

Born and raised in the small town of
Holly Hill, South Carolina, during his
teenager years, Brian Sewell traveled a bit
and fell madly in love but things fell apart.
That started his well. Poetry became the
outlet for his pain.

As time passed, he grew older and the
blinders that he believes many people
carry, fell from his eyes. He gained a
mentor at the age of 24 who encouraged
his quest for knowledge. The well now
overflows.

Publishing was always his dream, so he

finally decided it was time to publish his work at the encouragement of a special woman in his life.

"I never thought I'd be a published author but dreams do indeed come true and I am living proof..."   *The Native*

www.ingramcontent.com/pod-product-compliance
Lightning Source LLC
Chambersburg PA
CBHW060626030426
42337CB00018B/3221